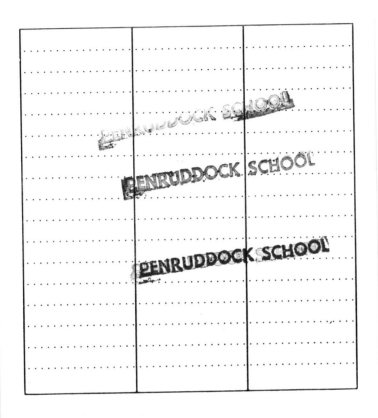

J531.3   OLLERENSHAW, C.

Wind-ups

Wind-ups

Chris Ollerenshaw and Pat Triggs
Photographs by Peter J Millard

Contents

A & C Black · London

What's in the toybox?

A few of the toys from this toybox are broken or have bits missing. When they worked properly they all moved or had moving parts. Can you see why they don't move any more?

Anything that moves – cars, bicycles, footballs, even people – needs energy. If you rush about a lot someone might say 'You're being energetic'. But even when you are sitting down and being quiet you are using energy.

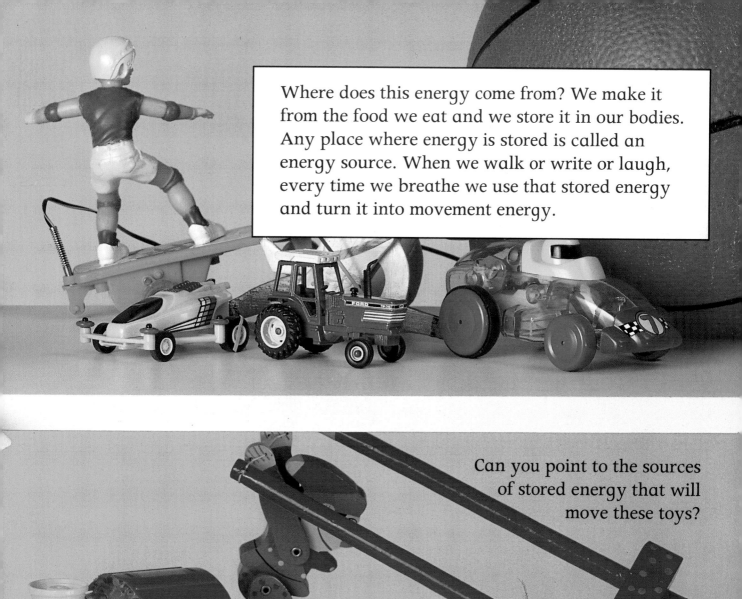

Where does this energy come from? We make it from the food we eat and we store it in our bodies. Any place where energy is stored is called an energy source. When we walk or write or laugh, every time we breathe we use that stored energy and turn it into movement energy.

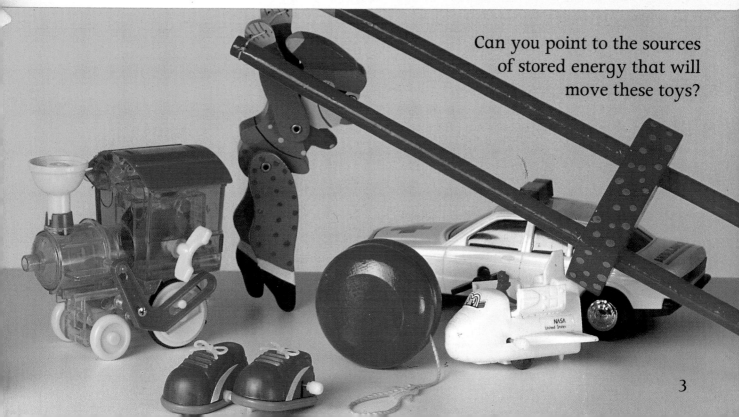

Can you point to the sources of stored energy that will move these toys?

3

Stretchy and springy

People have found how to use different kinds of energy sources to make things move.

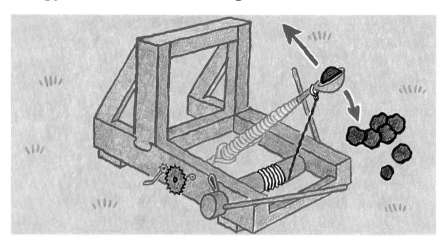

Can you picture in your mind how these war machines work? There is something they have both got in common.

They work because parts of them can be stretched and let go. Materials that have stretchiness or springiness can be used to provide sources of energy.

4

Some tree branches, (look at the tree on the right), are springy and bendy. Scientists have found out how to make artificial materials – like foam rubber – which are similar to the ones in nature. Some materials are naturally bouncy and elastic, like rubber which we get from trees.

Can you think of any other natural or artificial materials that are stretchy or springy?

A powerful energy source

How does this simple catapult work? A stone is put into the sling. Then the sling is stretched and pulled back. When it is stretched, the catapult is an energy source. The energy is held in the tightly-stretched sling and in the stone.

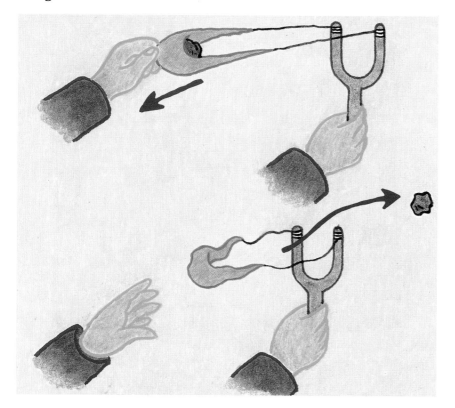

If the sling is released all that held energy is changed into movement energy as the sling snaps back and the stone goes flying through the air.

Being such a powerful energy source makes the catapult a dangerous weapon. Early hunters used slings and catapults to kill animals for food.

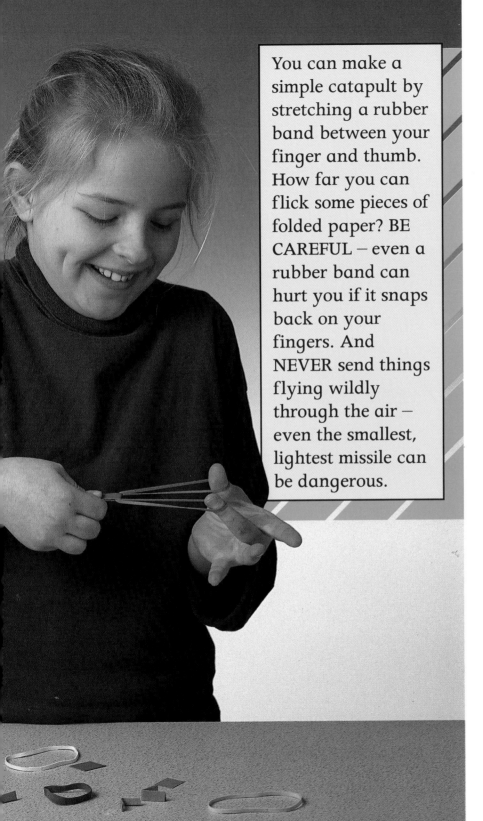

You can make a simple catapult by stretching a rubber band between your finger and thumb. How far you can flick some pieces of folded paper? BE CAREFUL – even a rubber band can hurt you if it snaps back on your fingers. And NEVER send things flying wildly through the air – even the smallest, lightest missile can be dangerous.

Can you see how this machine works?

Bouncing and squashing

The energy that makes this jack-in-the box work is held in a squeezed up cube. What kind of material do you think the cube is made of?

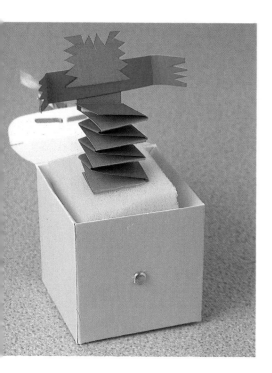

To find, out, collect together some balls like these made of different materials. Test how high they bounce. Why do you think some bounce higher than others?

Now squeeze each ball in your hand. Are some harder to squash than others? Do some spring back more easily than others? What does this tell you about the type of material you'd need to use inside the jack-in-the-box?

You could make your own jack-in-the-box. How could you use the stretchiness in a rubber band to allow the lid to lift so that your 'jack-in-the-box' figure can spring up?

9

Holding and releasing energy

Look at this toy acrobat. You can control the way it moves by the amount of energy you put into squeezing the poles. The harder you squeeze at the bottom the tighter the string is stretched at the top. As you relax your squeezing the string loosens and twists.

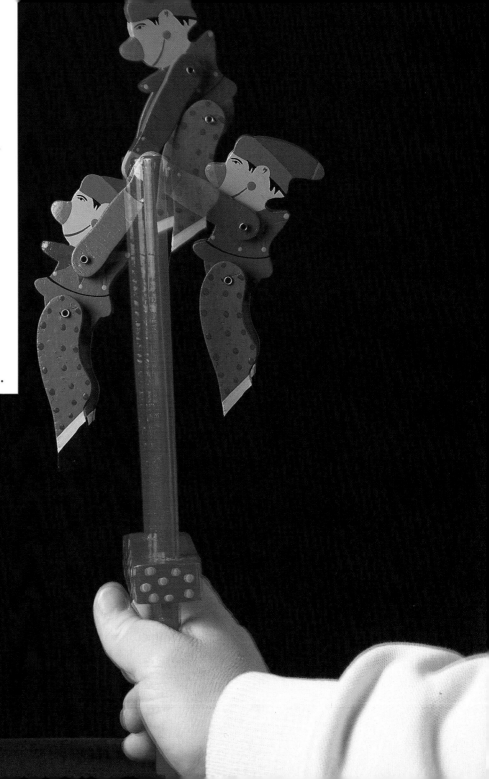

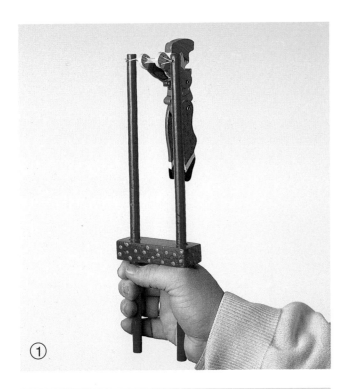

①

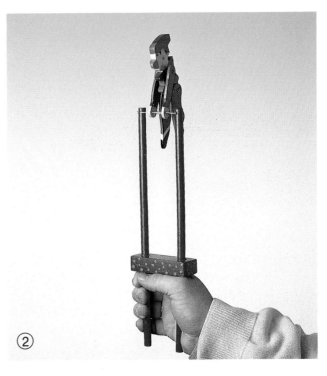

②

Tell the story of exactly what is happening to the poles, the string and the acrobat in each of these pictures.

③

Making metal bounce

Some materials are naturally stretchy or springy. Metal isn't, but it can be made to be.

If you twist metal round and round you can make it into something which will stretch and bounce back. You can make a SPRING.

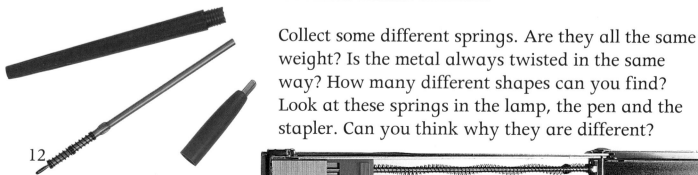

Collect some different springs. Are they all the same weight? Is the metal always twisted in the same way? How many different shapes can you find? Look at these springs in the lamp, the pen and the stapler. Can you think why they are different?

Why it is useful to be able to make springs out of metal? Try making a spring yourself by twisting some metal wire. Could you use it to help you make a jumping toy?

This toy works by using a metal spring. The spring is hidden. Can you work out where it is and what is happening? How does the animal collapse and then stand up again? How does it work?

Try to draw a picture of what is inside the base.

Springs for comfort

Springiness makes life much more comfortable. Travelling along a bumpy road in this cart you would feel every jolt and jar. The wheels are rimmed with wood and metal.

This carriage was designed with the body hanging from straps. The straps acted like springs to cushion the passengers from the worst bumps. The seats were padded which made them softer and a bit bouncy.

Modern cars have springs built into their design. Not all the springs are coiled. Leaf springs are flat. If you could look underneath modern cars and trucks you would see that lots of them have leaf springs built into them.

The wheels on modern cars are covered with springy rubber tyres. There are springs in the seats too. Travelling along the same road today would be much more comfortable.

If you have a bicycle, look under the saddle. And think about why some bikes have wide rubber tyres and some are narrow.

See if you can discover some more ways we use springiness and stretchiness to make our lives more comfortable. Look at the mattress on your bed. Does it have springs inside it? It might be made of springy rubber or foam. What about carpets, armchairs and sofas, or even camp beds and garden loungers?

Making things move

You can combine stretchiness with twisting or winding up to make another energy source.

Try making this toy. You will need: a plastic bottle, a rubber band, some small pieces of dowel or pencil and a bead.

Make a hole in the base of the bottle and thread the rubber band through. Slip a piece of dowel or pencil through the loop of the band poking through the base to stop it slipping out.

Pull the band through the neck of the bottle. You could cut the bottle in half first, as the girl on the right of the picture has done. Try out different rubber bands to find the right size for your machine.

Now thread the rubber band through the bead. The bead should sit in or on the neck of the bottle. If your bottle is in two halves, fit the top half into the bottom half.

Slip another piece of dowel or pencil through the loop of the band that is poking through the bead. The dowel or pencil is now fixed to the bead like a propellor. The bead helps the propellor to turn easily. What else could you use to do the same job?

Now turn the propellor round and round so that it twists the rubber band. When you think you have wound it up enough turn the bottle on its side, let the propellor go and watch how your machine moves. What is making it move like that?

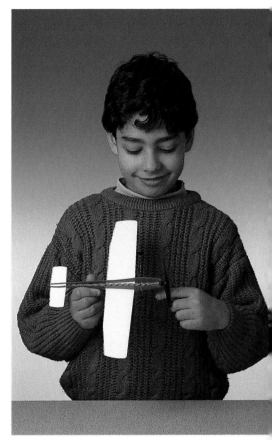

This plane from the toybox works in a similar way. Energy is being held in the twisted rubber band. When you release the rubber band the plane travels through the air with its movement energy. When the band has unwound, there is no more held energy to pass on and the plane will stop.

Keeping movement going

Spinners like this one do a lot of winding and unwinding. All you need to make a spinner is a circle of card with two holes in it and a length of thin string or cord.

Thread the string through the two holes so that you have a loop. Then tie the ends of the string together. Hold one end of the loop in each hand and wind up the string by flicking the spinner over and over.

When the string is nicely twisted, pull your hands apart and tighten the string. The spinner should whizz round as the string unwinds. You can keep it going by pulling on the string before it is completely unwound and then relaxing again. Do this during each spin.

What is making the spinner work? It is getting most of its energy from the work you are doing with your muscles, but the twisted string is holding some energy, too. Did you notice that you had to work harder to get your spinner going than to keep it spinning? Can you think why?

Ask your friends to try. Watch what they do. Get your spinner going and then stop pulling and relaxing the string. What happens? Does the spinner stop straight away?

Did your spinner make a noise when it was whizzing round? If it did, it was because the stored energy in the wound-up string changed into movement energy and into noise when you released it.

Explore making more spinners. Try using different sizes, shapes and materials. What differences do you notice each time you change the design?

Winding things up

Lots of wind-up toys need a key. What do you think happens inside a toy like this one (picture A) when you turn the key?

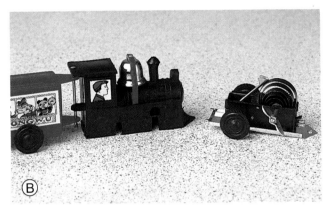

If you could take a wind-up toy apart (picture B), you could see what happens.

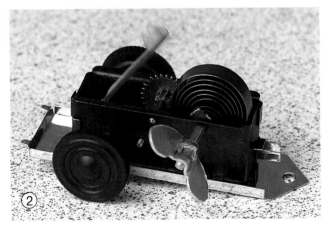

The key is turning in a coil of metal. This is another kind of spring. Look at the spring when it's wound up and ready to go (picture 1). Look at it when it has run down (picture 2). What changes did you see?

When you turn the key of a wind-up toy and tighten the spring you are putting energy into it which it can store. The spring unwinds as the toy uses the energy to move.

See if you can collect some wind-up toys together and watch how they move. Wind up each toy as much as you can. Measure how far each one travels.

Which goes the furthest? Why do some travel further than others? How long does it take each toy to cover the same distance? Which is the fastest? Which is the slowest? What affects the speed?

Try the toys on different surfaces. How well do each of them work on wood, carpet, earth and concrete?

Nearly 400 years ago, clockmakers began to use a wind-up spring as the energy source for their clocks. This made clocks tell the time accurately. It also meant at a later time that clocks could be smaller and people could wear them as watches.

Look at this spring-driven watch. It uses gear wheels and levers to make a movement which measures the time and moves the hands.

The same kind of movement was used to make toys that moved. For a long time toys like this were known as clockwork toys.

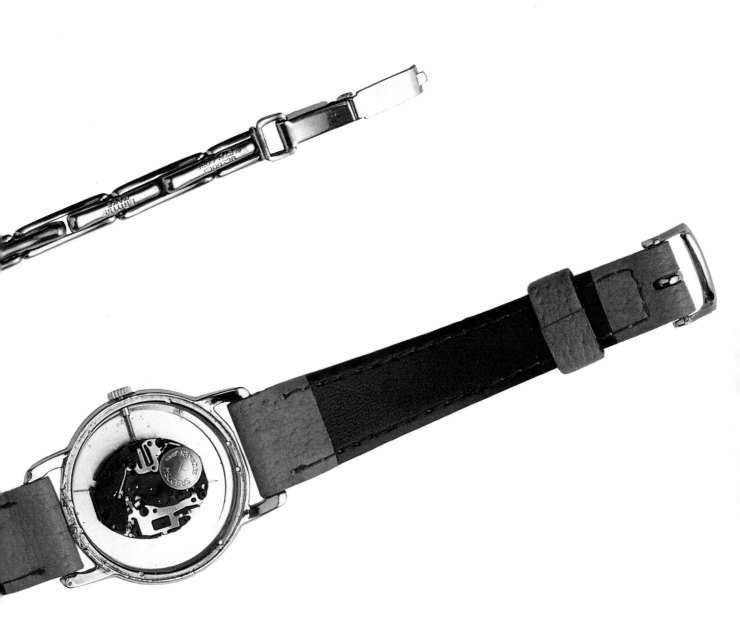

Sixty years ago the first quartz clock was made.
It was very accurate and didn't need winding up.
Nowadays lots of people have quartz watches, like
this one, that get their energy from batteries.

Winding up, winding down

Before clocks had wind-up springs they were worked by winding up of a different kind.

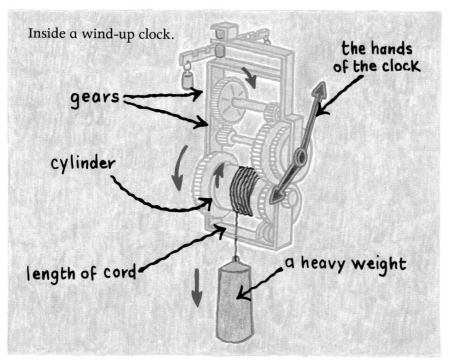

Inside a wind-up clock.

gears

cylinder

length of cord

the hands of the clock

a heavy weight

A length of cord wound round and round a cylinder was attached to a heavy weight. The weight hung free so that it could fall. Its fall was controlled by gears so it fell in jerks each one making a tick. The weight falling moved all the clockwork and the hands. When the weight reached the end of the cord someone had to wind it up again to the top.

Pendulum clocks worked in much the same way. Weights fell down and had to be wound back to the top for the clock to go on working.

You can watch how things fall. Put some things on the edge of a table and push them off. (Choose things that won't break!) Watch what happens.

It is gravity that pulls things downwards. Look at page 24 again. The designers of wind-up clocks knew about gravity. They knew that the weight would move downwards and that once it reached the ground the clock would stop, even if there was still cord left to unwind.

In wind-up clocks, the weight and the cord are in just the right position to hold energy. The held energy becomes movement energy as the weight falls and turns the cylinder.

Using gravity

You can use gravity to help you to design another kind of spinner like this one. You won't have to keep pulling it. It will keep moving for quite a long time.

Find or make a ball and thread a cord right through its centre. You could attach some tassels or fringes to it as well if you like.

Tie the cord to a pin or hook so that the ball hangs down. Twist the cord round and round. Before you let it go decide what sort of energy you think it has. Let go and watch what happens.

How long will your ball keep spinning? What happens to the tassels?

Try hanging the ball from different lengths of cord. What difference does this make? Try different sizes and weights of ball. What happens?

Gravity affects the way things move. Look what happens if the acrobat toy is turned on its side and the bottom of the poles squeezed. In this position gravity is not helping the acrobat to swing through the poles.

A yoyo is another sort of wind-up toy that needs gravity to work properly. The yoyo unwinds from the spool. When it reaches the end of the string it can bounce back and wind itself up again. Some of the movement energy it gets from going down goes into the bounce back.

As you move your hand up and down you are giving the yoyo more energy to keep it going – just as you did with the spinner. The spool is also falling down because of gravity.

Try one more toy from the toybox. Can you work out the energy changes when you bounce a rubber ball?

Make a moving roundabout

Now you know something about energy.

You know we need energy to make things happen. You know energy can be held in things like springs and rubber bands when they are in a position for that energy to be used. You know that energy is held and can be transferred to movement energy to make things happen.

You know how gravity plays a part. We use the knowledge that its downward pull makes all things fall when we design machines. You know how useful some materials can be – and about stretching and releasing, tightening and loosening, squeezing and letting go, winding and unwinding.

Now you can use some of those ideas to help you make a moving roundabout. The blueprint on pages 30 and 31 will help you.

Index

A CIP catalogue record for this book is available from the British Library.

ISBN 0–7136–3357–3

First published 1991 by A & C Black (Publishers) Ltd
35 Bedford Row, London, WC1R 4JH

Reprinted 1992, 1993, 1994

Text © 1991 Chris Ollerenshaw and Pat Triggs
All photographs © Peter J Millard except p 7 and p 14 Mary Evans Picture Library.

Model and blueprint by David Ollerenshaw
Ilustrations by Dennis Tinkler
Designed by Michael Leaman

Filmset by August Filmsetting, Haydock, St Helens
Printed in Belgium by Proost International Book Production

Acknowledgements

The photographer, authors and publishers would like to thank the following people whose help and co-operation made this book possible: Belinda, Joanne, Juliette, Beini, Tony, Joseph, Ernest and the staff and pupils of Avondale Park Primary School, Royal Borough of Kensington and Chelsea.

Roundabout

Build this working model using a wind-up motor of your own design. You will need an upturned paper plate measuring 18 cm across for the base and an upturned, brightly-coloured paper cup for the centre support. The whole revolving top of the model is carried on one lollipop stick. If your motor can turn this stick the model will come to life.

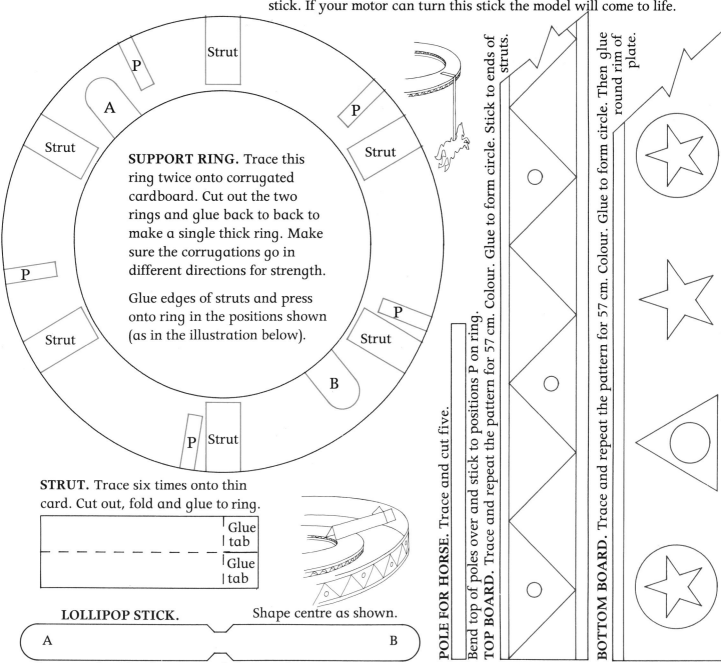

Strut

P

A

Strut

P

Strut

P

P

Strut

B

P   Strut

SUPPORT RING. Trace this ring twice onto corrugated cardboard. Cut out the two rings and glue back to back to make a single thick ring. Make sure the corrugations go in different directions for strength.

Glue edges of struts and press onto ring in the positions shown (as in the illustration below).

STRUT. Trace six times onto thin card. Cut out, fold and glue to ring.

Glue tab

Glue tab

Shape centre as shown.

LOLLIPOP STICK.

A   B

Glue to underside of ring. Match letter to letter.

POLE FOR HORSE. Trace and cut five.

Bend top of poles over and stick to positions P on ring.

TOP BOARD. Trace and repeat the pattern for 57 cm. Colour. Glue to form circle. Stick to ends of struts.

BOTTOM BOARD. Trace and repeat the pattern for 57 cm. Colour. Glue to form circle. Then glue round rim of plate.

30 (Think about your motor before glueing.)

TRACE these shapes onto card or paper as directed.
CUT along all solid black lines.

FOLD along all dotted black lines (score along dotted lines with an electrical screwdriver before folding.)

GREEN lines show where to glue. **RED** lines give ideas for decoration.

ROOFING. Trace and cut out of thick paper. Colour before glueing. Do not glue roof to model. Drop into place.

HORSE. Trace and cut five out of thick white paper. Leave white. Glue to poles.

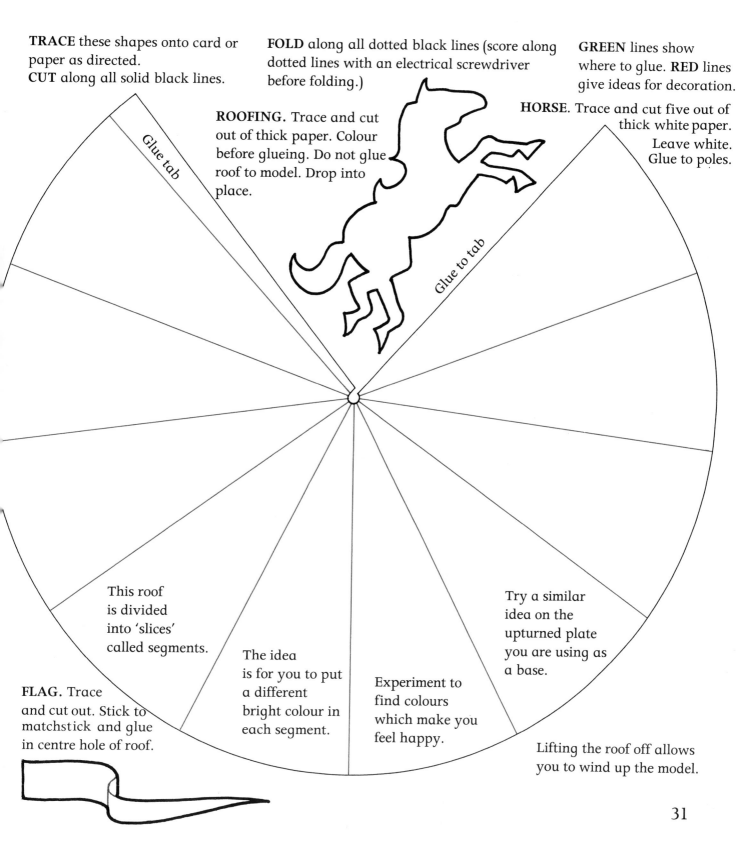

Glue tab

Glue to tab

This roof is divided into 'slices' called segments.

The idea is for you to put a different bright colour in each segment.

Experiment to find colours which make you feel happy.

Try a similar idea on the upturned plate you are using as a base.

FLAG. Trace and cut out. Stick to matchstick and glue in centre hole of roof.

Lifting the roof off allows you to wind up the model.

31

Notes for teachers and parents

Each title in this series promotes investigation as a way of learning about science and being scientific. Children are invited to try things out and think things through for themselves. It's very important for the children to handle the materials mentioned in the books, as only by making their own scientific explorations can they construct an explanation that works for them.

Each Toybox Science book is structured so that it follows a planned cycle of learning. At the **orientation** stage, with a starting point which mixes familiar and unfamiliar materials, children draw on their previous experience to organise their ideas. **Exploration** encourages clarification and refining of ideas and leads to **investigation**. At this stage children are testing and comparing, a process which leads to developing, restructuring and replacing ideas. **Reviewing** is an important part of this stage and can occur at the end or throughout as appropriate. Children discuss what they have found out and draw conclusions, perhaps using recorded data. Finally, open-ended problems provide opportunities for **application** of acquired knowledge and skills.

In writing these books we drew on our practical experience of this cycle to select and sequence activities, to frame questions, to make strategic decisions about when to introduce information and specialized vocabulary, when to summarise and suggest recording. The use of industrial applications and the introduction of a historical perspective are to encourage the linkage of ideas.

The **blueprint** at the end of each book encourages children to apply their learning in a new situation. There is no 'right' answer; the problem could be solved in any number of ways and children should be left to find their own.

The **national curriculum**: the first four books in the series are concerned with energy, forces and the nature of materials explored within an overall notion of movement and how things work.

WIND-UPS

Ideas about stored energy and energy changes are explored in a variety of ways in this book. The term 'wind-up' is used to explore 'springiness' in general (not merely a spring wound up by means of a key).

The book invites exploration of materials and their properties in relation to their use. Investigating the stretchiness and springiness of materials and the way this can be held and released (p 6 onwards) is followed by exploring twisted materials to see how winding stores energy (p 12 – jumping frog).

Twisting and stretchiness are combined in an activity which creates movement (kinetic) energy and a rewinding process (pp 16/17 spinner). Winding and unwinding (pp 18/19) leads to the wind-up spring and key (pp 20/21). Finally the book considers the use of the force of gravity in a system that uses potential energy (pp 24/25) and links ideas of gravity with energy in twisting materials (pp 26/27 yoyo).

Resources
Children working with this book will be best supported by:

- A collection of assorted materials similar to those mentioned in the book.
- A resource box of tools and basics like paper fasteners, rubber bands, etc and everyday junk materials (to be stored and labelled to allow children to access them independently.)
- The availability of construction kits.
- Collections of toys and real world objects similar to those mentioned in the book.
- Books and pictures related to the topic of the book to support enquiry and investigation.
- Visits to places where they can see industrial applications, current and historical.